Y0-DJM-487

Animals of the World
Consultant Editor Sir Maurice Yonge CBE FRS

Penguins

Ralph Whitlock

RAINTREE CHILDRENS BOOKS
Milwaukee · Toronto · Melbourne · London

U.S. edition text, copyright © 1977, Raintree Publishers
Limited

First published in the United States of America by Raintree
Publishers Limited, 1977

Distributed to the Book Trade by the Two Continents
Publishing Group, 30 East 42nd Street, New York, 10017

All rights reserved. No part of this book may be reproduced or
utilized in any form or by any means, electronic or mechanical,
including photocopying, recording, or by any information
storage and retrieval system, without permission in writing from
the Publisher. Inquiries should be addressed to Raintree
Publishers Limited, 205 West Highland Avenue, Milwaukee,
Wisconsin 53203.

Library of Congress Number: 77-14042

2 3 4 5 6 7 8 9 0 81 80

Printed in England by Loxley Brothers Ltd.
Library bound in the United States of America.

First published in the United Kingdom by Wayland Publishers
Ltd., 1977
Copyright © 1977, Wayland Publishers Ltd.

Library of Congress Cataloging in Publication Data

Whitlock, Ralph.
Penguins.

(Animals of the world)
Bibliography: p.56
Includes index.
SUMMARY: Describes the physical characteristics and habits
    of penguins, focusing on the Adélie penguin, the most common
    type on the Antarctic continent.
1. Penguins—Juvenile literature. [1. Adélie penguin. 2.
    Penguins] I. Title. II. Series.
    QL696.S473W48 1977 598.4'41 77-14042
    ISBN 0-8172-1078-4 lib. bdg.

Paperback edition ISBN 0-8467-0403-x

Introduction

Most penguins spend all their lives in the snow, ice, and freezing waters of Antarctica around the South Pole, and most of the year they spend in the water. Few human beings have ever been to this cold wasteland, swept by blizzards, to see how the penguin survives in this bitter region. But we do know that the penguin is a truly amazing animal, able to travel thousands of miles in a year, taking good care of its young, living almost entirely on the little, shrimplike krill, and escaping from its enemies, the fierce leopard seal and the skua. In this book, we learn about the penguin and how it lives, and especially about the Adélie penguin, one of the only two species to live on the Antarctic mainland.

1
The Penguin Tribe

Imagine an Arctic scene, with polar bears on an iceberg and penguins in the sea. Is there anything wrong? Well, polar bears and penguins are never found near each other, except in zoos. Polar bears live in the Arctic, in the frozen wastes around the North Pole. Penguins live in Antarctica, the frozen regions around the South Pole. They have been around for 60 million years—birds that cannot fly.

True, some penguins do live in warmer countries. This Galapagos penguin lives in the Galapagos Islands, off the coast of South America and nearly on the equator. But the sea here is kept very cold by an ocean current from the south. It is also full of the food that penguins like to eat. You will not find any penguins living north of the equator.

There are eighteen species of penguin. Here we can see three of them—the King penguin, the Macaroni, and the Gentoo. These all breed on the islands in the cold and stormy ocean around Antarctica, not on the continent itself. The King penguin is the biggest of the three. It weighs up to 16 kg. (35 lb.) and stands 91 cm. (3 ft.) high. The Macaroni penguin, although it measures 71 cm. (28 in.), weighs only about 4 kg. (9 lb.). The Gentoo penguin is also about 71 cm. (28 in.) long but weighs some 5½ kg. (12 lb.). Some penguins are fatter than others. In the thick clumps of grass of the barren sub-Antarctic islands, these penguins nest in huge colonies. But they stay there only to nest. Their true home is the sea.

Only two penguins breed on the main continent of Antarctica, the Adélie and the Emperor. The commonest is the Adélie, a small penguin, 71 cm. (28 in.) long and weighing about 5 kg. (11 lb.). You can see it in many zoos. It is black on the head, back, and wings, and white on the chest, like a little man in a tuxedo. On land it usually stands upright and waddles about with its head in the air.

Most penguins look something like the Adélie. Some, such as the Jackass penguin and these Magellanic penguins, have striped patterns of black and white. Others, such as the Macaroni and Rockhopper, have crests of yellow feathers just above their eyes.

10

This is a tiny Fairy penguin on the water. These are found in seas south of Australia. They have blue rather than black plumage. The big Emperor penguin and the smaller King penguin have yellow or cream fronts for camouflage. Think of a penguin swimming under water: a dangerous leopard seal swimming above will hardly notice its dark back against the blackness below. An enemy swimming beneath is confused by the bright light of the sky, and may not see the penguin's light underparts.

2
In Ice and Snow

The Adélie penguin spends all its life amid ice and snow. In winter it lives in the cold sea, seldom moving far from the icebergs and ice floes. The wild Antarctic storms and the high waves they create hardly bother the penguins. They swim under water as often as on the surface. Krill is their main food—shrimp-like animals occurring in such vast numbers in Antarctic seas that they also provide food for the great rorqual whales. Penguins also eat fish and squid.

As you can see, the penguin's body is well suited to life in the sea. It is streamlined for swimming, like a fish or a seal. Instead of large wings, which would get in the way and act as brakes, the penguin's wings are pretty small— more like the flippers of a seal than bird wings. In water they become strong paddles.

Penguins are also safe from the cold and wet. Their thick, oily feathers are small and tightly packed. There are as many as 60 to 70 per square inch (12 per square centimeter), giving the bird a good, watertight covering. Beneath them are layers of down and fat and a very thick skin. Penguins are so well insulated that even in Antarctica they sometimes become too hot. They may stand still for a few minutes, fluffing out their feathers to let the body heat escape.

The penguin's webbed feet are not protected
by feathers. So, to live on the ice without its feet
freezing, the penguin has two body tempera-
tures. Most of its body has the same high
temperature as that of other birds. But the
temperature of its feet and flippers is much
lower, nearer to that of a cold-blooded snake or
fish. On land, the penguin waddles awkwardly.
Its torpedo shape, which serves it so well at sea,

is not so good for life on land. Its short legs are
too near its tail. It has to stand upright and take
very short steps, which make it look comical to us.
These penguins are in a hurry. Perhaps they are
being chased. They have flopped down on their
stomachs to help themselves along with their
wings, just as if they were swimming. They are
tobogganing. Penguins can reach a good speed
by tobogganing, especially over smooth ice.

3
The Search for Land

For more than half the year, the Adélie penguin lives in the polar seas. But, of course, it has to come ashore for nesting. Penguins have been studied mostly on land. We know very little about their life in the ocean. Adélie penguins arrive at their breeding grounds on mainland Antarctica in October. How far do they come— 80 km. (50 mi.)?—we can hardly know. Not long ago two tagged birds were found to have journeyed 3,540 km. (2,200 mi.) from where they had been marked eleven months before!

October is the Antarctic spring, like April in

the northern hemisphere. When the penguins arrive for nesting, they often find the sea still frozen a long way from shore. Sometimes they have to travel for great distances across the ice. But they dare not nest there: in summer the ice may break up and float away as icebergs. Sometimes the penguins arrive at the edge of the ice to find a wall that is quite high. They swim back and come in again at speed, leaping out of the water and scrambling to the top of the ice shelf. They can jump about 1.8 m. (6 ft.) this way. Next begins the search for a nesting ground.

Penguins all nest in large colonies. They are social birds. Even in the winter when they are at sea they move about in flocks. There is safety in numbers. The odds against being seized by an enemy are fairly small! Many species of penguin nest on tiny islands, so they have to crowd together. On Dassen Island, off the coast of South Africa, enormous numbers of Jackass penguins have nested for centuries, until they have worn deep paths in the solid rock.

Adélie penguins have plenty of space in the 14 million sq. km. ($5\frac{1}{2}$ million sq. mi.) of Antarctica. All the same, they nest in huge colonies known as "rookeries." Some rookeries have more than a million pairs of penguins in them. If you look back to the picture at the beginning of this chapter, you will see an icy hillside covered with black dots. Each dot is a group of penguins in their rookery.

23

When nesting time comes, the adult males, who have nested before, arrive first. They find their old nesting sites and start to repair them. This they do by collecting a heap of stones. The air is filled with the loud screams, barks, and squeals of squabbling penguins. Although they gather in such huge rookeries, penguins are quarrelsome birds. And it is easier to steal stones than to find your own!

A week or two later, the females and the younger males arrive. The younger males, who have not bred before, have to find new sites on the edge of the colony. The females go straight to their old nesting sites. There they hope to find the same male with whom they mated last year. And they hope he has a good pile of stones. They will not mate with him till he has. This Adélie penguin is working hard to build up his collection in time.

When the penguins arrive at their rookeries, the ground is still frozen, and the sites are often covered with snow. If they can, the birds choose sites on higher ground. The snow is not so deep, and perhaps the rock is already exposed.

Both male and female help to build the nest. They scrape a hole with their powerful feet and claws and line it with the stones. If the stones are frozen to the ground, the birds will sit

on them till the ice melts. They need the lining
of stones to keep the eggs from rolling away, and
to raise them safely above any floods caused by
melting snow.

In the heart of a penguin rookery, each
nesting pair occupies a territory of about one
square meter (1 sq. yd.). In this way each bird
sitting on its nest is just out of pecking range
of its next-door neighbor.

Adélie penguins take their time in settling down to life as parents. They spend about four weeks in courtship before the first egg is laid. These are very noisy weeks in the rookery. The birds squeal, croak, bark, croon, and make all kinds of noises, according to their mood. When the males have found their nesting sites and are looking for their mates, they raise their beaks to the sky, flap their flippers, and make a loud, throbbing call. When the females have joined them, the pair together often raise their heads in the same way and "talk" to each other. They also wave their heads together, in a kind of swaying dance. From time to time they mate.

28

But sometimes the partners squabble. And always they have to guard against stealing by other penguins. Sometimes stones are stolen—sometimes even the female! Male penguins often make a threat display. They puff out their bodies toward the intruder and stare at him with glaring eyes, croaking loudly. If this fails they fight, pecking and shoving each other. At last the female is ready to start egg-laying. Adélie penguins generally lay two bluish white eggs, two or three days apart. The eggs in the huge rookeries are all laid within about three weeks, so that all the young chicks hatch at about the same time.

As soon as she has laid the second egg, the female returns to the sea to feed. Incubation is started by the male. He sits on the nest with the eggs balanced on top of his feet and pressed into his warm stomach. There he sits, on the cold Antarctic shore, often with blizzards raging around him, for a week to ten days. Then the female returns and takes over for a similar period. After that, the male and female change places every two or three days—at least, when things go well. Penguins can feed only in the sea, not on land. The female goes back to the sea first because her body has had the extra strain of producing eggs. But the male comes to the site a week or so before she does, and then has to wait a week or more before his next meal. If the ice is slow in breaking up, the female has to go a long way to find the sea, and she may come back late. Then, when it is the male's turn to go fishing, he may be too weak to finish the trip.

Although one of the two eggs was laid two
or three days after the other, they both hatch
at about the same time. This happens from 33 to
35 days after laying. As you can see, when the
chicks have dried off after hatching out of the
egg, they are covered with a silvery grey down.
The parents continue to take turns at
brooding—sitting on the nest for two or three

weeks, keeping the chicks warm. The other parent is away hunting. He or she comes back from time to time and feeds the chicks by regurgitation. The parent stores food in its crop, much as a pigeon does. When it returns to the nest, the baby bird puts its head right inside the parent's mouth and reaches down its throat for the food.

Within two or three weeks, the chicks are growing fast and need both parents to fetch food. The young leave their nests and form nurseries, or crèches, with 50 or 60 other chicks. An adult female, an "auntie" like this one, looks after the nursery. With their parents away, the chicks face many dangers. A terrible blizzard may blow up, burying them in snow drifts or freezing them to death. They may wander away and get lost. Worst of all are the attacks of skuas. These birds nest near the penguin colonies and feed on chicks and eggs. Sometimes they trick a parent into leaving its nest for a moment, and then snatch an egg or chick. Sometimes a group of skuas will attack a whole nursery. In the screams and confusion they usually manage to grab a few.

Parent penguins take very good care of their young. In a huge colony of a million birds, they go straight to the right nest. And when the young birds have joined a nursery, the parents usually know which are theirs. If they are not sure, the parents try a "feeding chase." They run away from the nursery. The chicks start to run after them, but those that don't belong soon give up. The right chicks go on chasing their parents. They know it is their only chance for a meal.

Gangs of young penguins are another danger. Hatched in earlier years, these are not yet old enough to nest. Sometimes they tear through the rookeries, scattering eggs and stomping on chicks. Others defend the nurseries against skuas when the parents are away.

Towards the end of the Antarctic summer, the chicks start to lose their down and grow feathers. Their first plumage is not quite like that of their parents. They do not have the white eyelids, so striking on their parents. And the chin is white, whereas that of their parents is black. At about eight weeks old, these young penguins are ready to look after themselves. They waddle off in groups to the sea and jump in. They need no swimming lessons; they are made for the water. Once their family is raised the parents, too, molt, or shed their feathers and grow bright new ones. During molting they stay behind in the rookery, worn out, and do not go to the sea to feed. They look very sloppy and unhappy.

4
Return to the Sea

When they have finished molting, first the young birds and then the adults waddle down to the sea and dive in. There the worst danger of all awaits them—the terrible leopard seals. The leopard seal is a slim, fierce animal, spotted like a leopard. Fortunately for the penguins, it is not very common, but one or two usually lurk just off the shore where the penguins are nesting. The seal eats fish, krill, and even carrion, but most of all it likes a meal of penguin. It can swim very fast and kills its prey with a single bite. It

skins the penguin by beating it against the water.

It is sad when a penguin survives all the dangers of nesting, only to get killed by a leopard seal. But since there are so many penguins, the chances of being caught are low. These penguins are lucky. The leopard seal is resting on the ice after a large meal, so they can pass near him without danger. Soon all the chattering penguins have left their nesting grounds. By early April the rookeries are quiet and empty.

Little is known of the life of the penguin during its six months or so at sea. Very few people visit Antarctica, and the number of those who have observed penguins under water is very small. It seems that Adélie penguins stay on pack ice all winter, because the krill is so plentiful there. Also the ice floes help them escape the dangerous leopard seals. When chased, penguins will leap into the air and skim

along the surface of the sea. Sometimes they find safety by landing on ice. It gives them a better chance, though leopard seals can also travel over ice.

Although they spend much time under water, penguins must come up to breathe. After taking a good breath, they can dive deep and often go fishing under ice floes. The Emperor penguin can stay under water for up to eighteen minutes.

5
The Emperor Penguin

The Emperor penguin is easily the largest species. It stands 1 m. (45 in.) high and weighs 27 to 29 kg. (60 to 65 lb.), nearly six times as much as the Adélie penguin. Like the Adélie it nests in the Antarctic, but it does so in mid winter. It incubates its eggs in the coldest season of the coldest place on earth.

In April, when the other penguins are moving north to escape the coming winter, the Emperor penguins are going south. They nest in large colonies; one contains more than 100,000 birds. While some of these colonies may be on the Antarctic continent or on nearby islands, they are often on sea ice. But the ice is safe: it will not break up during that cold season of the year.

Courtship and mating follow much the same pattern as with Adélie penguins. The female Emperor penguin lays only one pale green egg, weighing about 453 grams (1 lb.). As soon as it is laid, the male takes charge of it. He puts it on his feet and wraps a fold of skin around it. Then he stands up to incubate it—for two months! Emperor penguins do not build nests. The female then sets off over the ice to find the open sea. Sometimes she has to walk for 96 to 145 km. (60 to 90 mi.). It is much too far to run a shuttle service, as the Adélie penguins do.

So the male has to hatch the egg on his own. There he stands, with the temperature often sinking to −60°C (−76°F). All the time he is using up the fat stored in his body. He loses about 120 grams (4 oz.) a day. Fortunately, they are not as quarrelsome as the Adélies. They do not mark out territories and threaten each other. In the winter blizzards, the incubating Emperors huddle close together for warmth.

At the end of two months, in July, the females return, and the eggs begin to hatch. The female takes over, holding the chick on her feet just as the male has been doing. In her crop she has a good supply of sea food. The males, weighing only half what they did when they came to the nesting site, tramp off to the sea. They feed well and come back with a crop full of food for the chicks three or four weeks later.

From this point on, the father and mother penguins take turns collecting sea food for the chicks. By January or February, in the middle of the Antarctic summer, the youngsters are ready to make their first journey to the sea. By this time the journey is not so long, for the summer has melted much of the sea ice. The parents go with the chicks to molt.

6
The
Future of the Penguin

The first southern explorers killed and ate many penguins and their eggs. So did the crews of whaling ships that anchored in the island havens. Few people landed on the Antarctic continent until the present century. By then, people were more interested in protecting wild creatures. Today Antarctica is one great nature reserve. Most penguins, especially the Adélie, seem safe. Some, including the Emperor, may even be increasing.

The penguins that nest farther north, nearer to civilized countries, are in the most danger, for example from cats and rats. An even worse threat comes from oil spilled at sea. Giant oil tankers now pass regularly around the Cape of Good Hope, at the southern tip of Africa. Some have been wrecked there, polluting the ocean. The picture on the right shows a Jackass penguin from a colony that nests on Dassen Island, near the Cape. They have suffered terribly from oil spills. Another threat comes from DDT and other insecticides. Although none is used anywhere near Antarctica, traces of them have still been found in the blood of penguins on the Antarctic mainland. The DDT must largely have been carried there in the bodies of the fish that penguins eat. When these chemicals are found above a certain level in the bodies of birds in temperate and tropical countries, they sometimes keep the eggs from hatching. This has not yet happened to penguins, but it could do so: and what a tragedy that would be.

Glossary

ANTARCTIC The frozen land of ice and snow around the South Pole.

BLIZZARD A snowstorm with strong winds.

CAMOUFLAGE Skin or outer covering that blends with the background.

CARRION The flesh of a dead animal, generally starting to decay.

CRECHE A nursery, a place where young creatures can stay while their parents are busy.

CROP Throat pouch for storing food.

DDT A powerful insecticide, or chemical for killing insects.

DOWN The fine, powdery feathers that are the first plumage of a baby bird.

FEEDING CHASE A chase that occurs when a parent penguin pretends to run away in order to get her chicks to follow her.

FLIPPER The front limb of a penguin or a seal, used as an aid in swimming.

ICE FLOES A flat mass of floating ice.

INCUBATION The process of hatching an egg by warming it.

KRILL Small, shrimplike creatures that live in countless millions in Antarctic seas and are the chief food of most penguins.

MOLT The process of shedding feathers and growing a new set.

PACK ICE Floating ice that has been broken up and has frozen together again.

PLUMAGE Feathers.

REGURGITATION The process, used by penguins, of feeding young from the contents of the crop.

ROOKERIES A name given to nesting colonies of penguins.

SKUAS Large, brown gull-like birds that feed on penguin eggs and young penguins.

TAGGED Marked with a tag by scientists.

TERRITORY An area of land (or water) regarded by an animal or bird as its own. It will drive other creatures away from its territory.

TOBOGGANING This word is used to describe the action of penguins sliding over smooth ice and pushing themselves along with their flippers.

Further Reading

Burton, Maurice, and Burton, Robert, editors. *The New International Wildlife Encyclopedia*. 21 vols. Milwaukee: Purnell Reference Books, 1980.

Eberle, Irmengard. *Penguins Live Here*. Garden City, N.Y.: Doubleday & Company, 1975.

Johnston, Johanna. *Penguin's Way*. Eau Claire, Wis.: E. M. Hale & Company, 1962.

Lauber, Patricia. *Junior Science Book of Penguins*. New York: Scholastic Book Services, 1972.

Mizumura, Kazue. *Emperor Penguins*. New York: Thomas Y. Crowell Company, 1969.

Penney, Richard L. *Penguins Are Coming*. New York: Harper & Row, 1969.

Thompson, David H. *The Penguin: Its Life Cycle*. New York: Sterling Publishing Company, 1974.

ACKNOWLEDGMENTS
The author and publisher would like to thank the following for their permission to reproduce copyright illustrations on the pages mentioned: N.H.P.A., endpapers, 8 (top), 8 (bottom), 10 (left), 10 (right), 11, 12, 16, 23, 24, 28, 31, 34, 38, 40, 44, 53, back of jacket; Ardea Photographics, 5, 9, 21, 32, 33, 36, jacket front; Daphne Machin Goodall, 6, 37, 50; Eric Hosking, 7; Bruce Coleman, 15 (top), 19, 20, 26, 29, 35, 41, 42; and Frank Lane 15 (bottom), 46 and 48.

Index